Alex Morss & Sean Taylor

FUNNY BUMS, FREAKY BEAKS

and other incredible creature features

illustrated by Sarah Edmonds

EDITIONS

For you, dear reader. Keep thriving in difference, not indifference.
A.M.

For my dad, Cavan Taylor, who has always encouraged curiosity.
(Please don't take this dedication as a comment on your bum. Or your beak.)
S.T.

For Leo and Matt.
S.E.

Published in 2021 by Welbeck Editions

An imprint of Welbeck Children's Limited,
part of Welbeck Publishing Group.
20 Mortimer Street, London W1T 3JW

Text © Alex Morss and Sean Taylor 2021
Illustrations © Sarah Edmonds 2021

Alex Morss and Sean Taylor have asserted their moral right to
be identified as the Authors of this Work in accordance with
the Copyright Designs and Patents Act 1988.

Sarah Edmonds has asserted her moral right to be identified
as the Illustrator of this Work in accordance with the
Copyright Designs and Patents Act 1988.

Managing Art Editor: Matt Drew
Associate Publisher: Laura Knowles

All rights reserved. No part of this publication may be
reproduced, stored in a retrieval system, or transmitted
in any form or by any means, electronically, mechanical,
photocopying, recording or otherwise, without the prior
permission of the copyright owners and the publishers.

A CIP catalogue record for this book is available from
the British Library.

ISBN 978-1-91351-904-9

Printed in Heshan, China

10 9 8 7 6 5 4 3 2 1

Contents

Funny and Freaky?	4
Strange Tails	6
Puzzling Toes	10
Odd Noses	14
Funny Bums	18
Freaky Beaks	22
Extraordinary Eyes	26
Perplexing Necks	30
Weird Ears	34
Terrific Teeth	38
Peculiar Tongues	42
Who's Missing?	46
Find Out More	48

Funny and Freaky?

Why do living things look so different? You might think some animals look funny, freaky, puzzling or peculiar, but their weird features have amazing stories.

This book explores the world of incredible creature features and why many of them are there for good reasons - and often surprising ones. What might seem odd to us is something that's *just right* for another animal. It helps them live better, have more babies and survive.

Tiny changes to the shape of an animal's body can bring benefits, and these are then passed down to their young. Over thousands of years, their strangeness can become more extreme, if being unusual makes those animals more successful.

This is called evolution, and it's why we see such extraordinary variation in how animals look and behave. Nature's diversity makes planet Earth a richer, more beautiful place.

So if animals look *different*, are they funny and freaky? If we open our eyes a bit wider, might we find a treasure chest of the most interesting creatures on planet Earth?

Read on and see what you think...

Strange Tails

I'm a famous blue bird-of-paradise.

I look my most beautiful when dangling upside down, wiggling my exotic bottom in the air and arching my tail wires.

Many stunning birds-of-paradise perform in our jungle. We buzz, chatter and sing exquisite songs. We dance. We wear feathery ornaments on our bodies and tails. Some of us even make our own forest stages and put on shows. We never do things simply if they can be done with style.

Of course, none of our impossibly impractical features help us fly or stay alive. If anything, they slow us down and make us easy for predators to spot. But never mind. The prettiest bird wins a mate and gets to be a dad. So the show goes on!

Now it's time to raise the curtain, ladies and gentlemen, and present some special guests with stunning tails...

Why would a **luna moth** want fancy-looking tail wings? They fly at night and no one can see them. Well, it protects them from becoming bat snacks. Bats listen for sound echoes when they hunt, and this clever moth's tail bounces back their calls in confusing ways. It tricks bats into missing their target.

A sting in the tail? Actually, no. It's not a real tail, but it has a few tricks... It's a pointy posterior and part of a **scorpion's** abdomen. At the end of it is this famous king of stings' needle-like venomous spine. But a scorpion's 'tail' also contains its bum and some light sensors which work like eyes. Many scorpions glow in the dark under ultraviolet moonlight. And they use these light sensors to spot other animals, decide where to stab them, and how much poison to inject.

Unlike most fish, a **tiger-tailed seahorse** has a tail with four flat sides. It's got some unique advantages. Square tails help seahorses resist injury. Their tails curl and grip onto sea grass, mangrove roots and coral reefs, even in strong ocean currents. This is important because seahorses have no tail fin and are poor swimmers. They are also used during courtship, when seahorses spin and dance holding onto each other's tails.

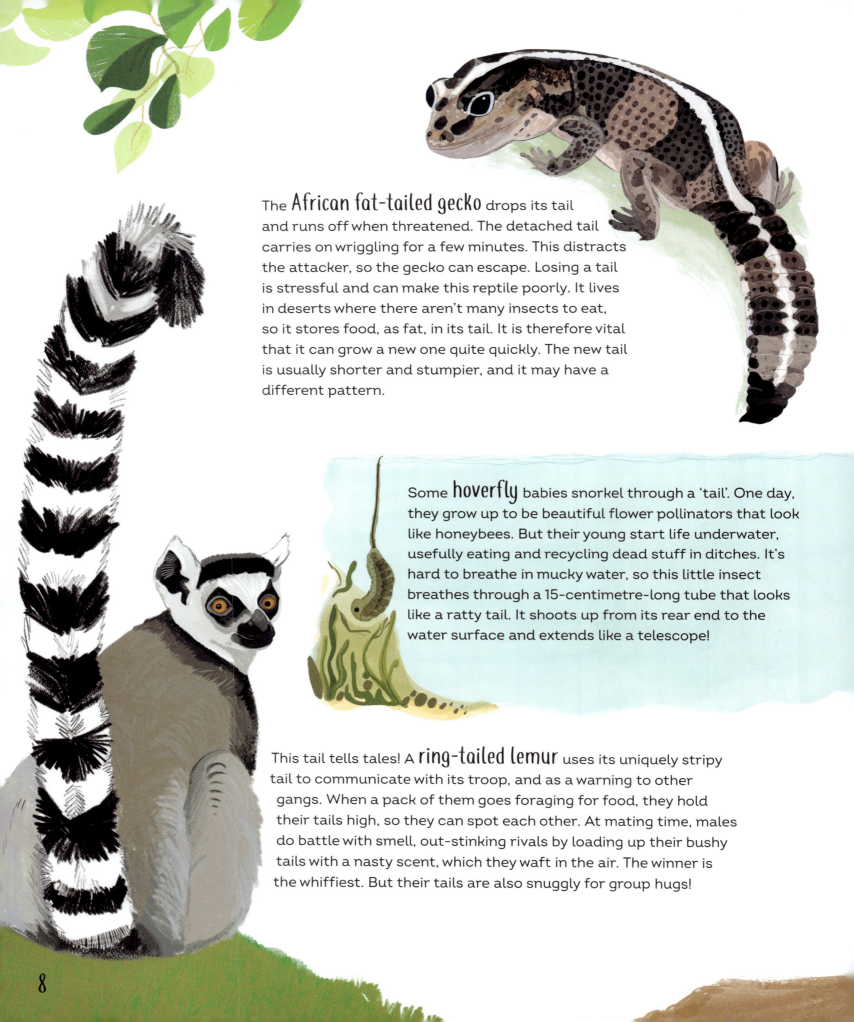

The **African fat-tailed gecko** drops its tail and runs off when threatened. The detached tail carries on wriggling for a few minutes. This distracts the attacker, so the gecko can escape. Losing a tail is stressful and can make this reptile poorly. It lives in deserts where there aren't many insects to eat, so it stores food, as fat, in its tail. It is therefore vital that it can grow a new one quite quickly. The new tail is usually shorter and stumpier, and it may have a different pattern.

Some **hoverfly** babies snorkel through a 'tail'. One day, they grow up to be beautiful flower pollinators that look like honeybees. But their young start life underwater, usefully eating and recycling dead stuff in ditches. It's hard to breathe in mucky water, so this little insect breathes through a 15-centimetre-long tube that looks like a ratty tail. It shoots up from its rear end to the water surface and extends like a telescope!

This tail tells tales! A **ring-tailed lemur** uses its uniquely stripy tail to communicate with its troop, and as a warning to other gangs. When a pack of them goes foraging for food, they hold their tails high, so they can spot each other. At mating time, males do battle with smell, out-stinking rivals by loading up their bushy tails with a nasty scent, which they waft in the air. The winner is the whiffiest. But their tails are also snuggly for group hugs!

How many tails do you need?
A **leafy seadragon** is covered by extraordinary tail-like leafy lobes. These are not for swimming. They camouflage this animal as he floats in kelp and seaweed. Unusually, the male carries eggs, not the female. He uses his real tail to help pump them out during birthing time.

Sea slugs and nudibranches, such as this **Willani sea slug**, are molluscs with fake 'tails'. These tiny creatures are among the most colourful animals in all the oceans. Their elaborate tail-like structures perform many roles. They are used for camouflage, defence against attackers, selecting a mate and even to breathe through. This particular one has a 'tail' that sparkles!

A **rattlesnake** is a timid animal. Her bite has venom, but she'll warn attackers first with her high-speed, rattling tail. The tip is made of hollow rings of keratin – the same material as fingernails. These bang together when three powerful muscles shake them, at up to 90 times per second. The rattling parts regularly snap off, but they regrow. Cold-blooded snakes can't escape in a hurry if it's chilly. So a scary rattle warning is a handy defence.

Puzzling Toes

Don't be puzzled. Let me explain!
My **gecko** toes are my superpower.

With them, I can whizz up walls. I can scuttle across glass. I can even hang upside down!

How? These wrinkly toes of mine have hundreds of folds in the skin. The folds are covered with tiny hairs. Each of them splits into even smaller bristles. And these give my toes so much sticking power, you may see me race across a ceiling.

What's more, when I want to travel the right way up, I can just change the angles of the hairs and turn their stickiness off.

If you think my toes are clever, look at the curious claws and toes on some of my friends...

Blue-footed boobies use their toes to dance the blue-footed-booby-boogie-woogie! They lift them up and down. They bow. They sway. They shuffle this way and that to show them off. Why? Because having bright blue feet shows you're a healthy booby. And that's a good way to attract a mate.

The **hairy frog** does a very unusual trick with her toes. If she senses danger, she pops her toe bones right out through her skin. Then it looks as if she has claws, like a cat. That's a nifty way of fending off an attacker.

A **two-toed earless skink** is a lizard. But it has the strangest of spindly little toes. Millions of years ago skinks used to get about on their feet. But then they found out that slithering like a snake is easier than walking. So now they wriggle and glide, they slink and slide and they only need tiny toes.

Mole crickets do a lot of digging. So it's handy that they have three pairs of legs with different-shaped toes on each. Their front feet are flat like spades and their toes are shaped like garden forks. This helps them burrow through soil at high speed to find worms, roots and leaves to eat.

A **jacana** has toes that stretch longer and wider than all of its body. With them, these brilliant birds can just about walk over water. They tiptoe over the leaves that float on marshes and lakes. This lets them catch the tastiest tiny water creatures, and they won't sink while eating their dinner!

Emperor penguins keep their bodies warm inside a cosy layer of blubber and feathers. But how do they stop their bare toes from freezing on minus 40°C Antarctic ice? The answer is some special veins and arteries, which change how blood flows into their toes. These cool their blood as it travels down, then warm the blood as it rises back up. It keeps the penguins' feet just above freezing.

A **Nubian ibex**, like all of its goat relatives, has toes shaped into cloven hooves. These amazing toes are flexible, with hard and soft parts. They give the ibex its daredevil ability to dash up and down steep mountains. So these cliff-hanging climbers grip onto rocks where few other creatures dare to tread.

A giant **harpy eagle** has the biggest talons of any living eagle. They use their fierce grip to snatch sloths, spider monkeys, snakes and macaws from the tree canopy. And their powerful talons have even been known to lift prey that weighs as much as themselves, such as small lambs and goats.

Three-toed sloths have long claws that make them clever climbers and skilful swimmers. They'll use their claws to swipe at an attacking jaguar or eagle. And, with their super-strong toes, they can hang for days in the treetops, where no predator can find them.

You can see why this chap's called a **pom pom crab**. His toes have tiny claws, just right for holding onto animals called anemones. A pom pom crab carries these around to sting attackers and catch food. They also help him show off his strength.

Odd Noses

I'm used to people staring at my lovely **saiga** nose.

It may look like a giant slug on the end of my face, but the truth is it's a rather special nose, even though I say so myself.

We saigas cross dry plains, looking for food, in large herds. That means we kick up clouds of dust. This nose is handy because it filters the dust from the air that we breathe.

What's more, it's a perfect nose for all kinds of weather. The large surface area inside my nose helps keep me cool in summer. Then, in winter, it warms cold air before it reaches my lungs.

There's one more thing my nose is good for – it helps me produce the low calls that let females know I'll make a good mate.

Now it's my pleasure to introduce you to some more creatures known for their magnificent noses...

Giant elephant shrews have long, pointy noses that move up, down, left, right and round and round. These little explorers use their helpful snouts when they're off looking for food and collecting bedding for their nests. With them, they can turn over leaves and dig out tasty termites, ants and seeds.

The eye-catching male **cecropia moth** has one of the oddest 'noses' around. How does he smell? With the feathery shapes sticking up from his head. These antennae give him an exceptionally strong sense of smell… and he needs it! He'll be looking for a mate after dark, so he'll have to find her by sniffing out her perfume. With his remarkable scent-finding ability, he can do that from over a kilometre away!

Honduran white bats use their noses to help them hear and find their way through thick jungle at night. They make high-pitch squeaks through their nostrils, turn them into sound beams with their 'nose leaf' and listen for the echoes coming back. It's called echolocation. These clever-nosed bats use it to find their favourite fig fruits, and the hidden roosts where they sleep during the day.

A **sawfish** looks as if it has stolen something from a carpenter's shed! And its long 'nose' is a practical tool. This seven-metre long ray lives in murky seas and muddy rivers where it can't rely on its eyesight for finding food. Instead, a sawfish uses its 'nose' to sense where other fish are. Then it hunts them down and chops them up with it too.

A **ghost shark** has a long, wobbly nose. It's covered in pores which sense movements and faint electrical currents made by tiny animals in the seabed. The shark also uses its underwater 'trunk' to sift through sand where its prey is hiding.

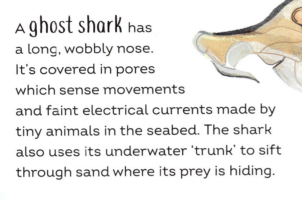

One of the largest and most powerful of all noses belongs to the **Asian elephant**. It's also amazingly useful. An elephant's trunk can push over a tree or pick up a twig. It can stretch up to feed on leaves and reach down to suck in gallons of water. Elephants use their trunks to spray themselves with cooling mud on hot days. They wave them to warn off attacking lions. What's more, their trunks have more scent detectors than any other known animal organ. So elephants can sniff out danger, food and water for kilometres around.

How would you like to look like this? A male **proboscis monkey** has a giant, floppy nose. Believe it or not, it's there to help him find a mate. Females like a male who's good at making noisy calls. A male's big nose has an echo chamber inside, which makes his calls louder. The larger his nose is, the louder he can honk, roar and snarl.

A nose is sometimes called a 'hooter', and that's a good description when it comes to an **elephant seal**. A male's whopping nose can make thunderous sounds that scare off rivals. This means his nose helps him defend his territory and win females to mate with. An elephant seal's huge hooter is handy in other ways, too. During the breeding season, a male won't feed for many days, but his nostrils can soak up moist air, which quenches his thirst.

This handsome snout belongs to a **long-beaked echidna**. Its long nose contains 2,000 electroreceptors. It uses these to sense movement and sniff out ant and termite nests. Inside an echidna's pointy nose is a sticky tongue ideal for lapping up little insects. When swimming, it sticks its snout up out of the water, like a snorkel, so it can breathe!

Here's a **star-nosed mole**. Why would you want a nose that looks like that? Well, it's the most sensitive nose of any mammal. As the mole tunnels through wet soil in darkness, she can just about 'see' with her nose! Her nose's 100,000 nerves can sense the slightest of smells and the tiniest of vibrations. This means she is brilliant at finding her way to food. In fact, her sniffer can even smell what's underwater!

Funny Bums

What are you laughing at? My **bum**?

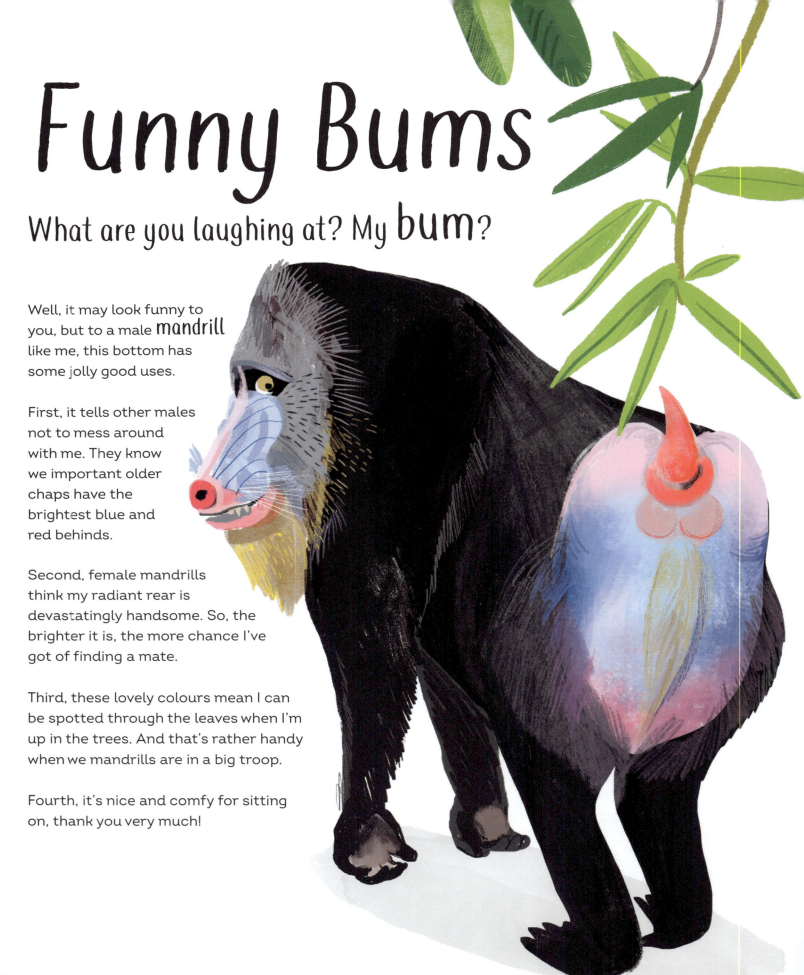

Well, it may look funny to you, but to a male **mandrill** like me, this bottom has some jolly good uses.

First, it tells other males not to mess around with me. They know we important older chaps have the brightest blue and red behinds.

Second, female mandrills think my radiant rear is devastatingly handsome. So, the brighter it is, the more chance I've got of finding a mate.

Third, these lovely colours mean I can be spotted through the leaves when I'm up in the trees. And that's rather handy when we mandrills are in a big troop.

Fourth, it's nice and comfy for sitting on, thank you very much!

Here are some other animals who have remarkably clever rear ends...

Manatees have marvellously useful bottoms. They can move around underwater by farting! They get gassy from munching on seaweed and greens. So they store up the gas to make themselves float. Or they get rid of it to make themselves sink. When they pass wind, the explosion of bubbles can even help them blast along!

An **eastern spotted skunk** may have the smelliest bum of all. He'll make sure you know, by doing a handstand and waving it in the air! It's a warning. If a predator comes closer, he squirts a terribly stinky, oily perfume from scent glands hidden in his bottom. This scares the visitor away. The liquid stings if it gets in the eyes, and the pong stays for days!

This is a baby **planthopper**. These wondrous bugs can squeeze sparkly spikes out of their backsides. They look like startling firework displays, and put off attackers. Their prickles also act like parachutes if a pretty little planthopper falls off a branch.

Would you like light to shine out from your behind? It does if you're a **firefly**. This beetle has a useful, glow-in-the-dark rear end. She winks her light to find the right mate. Her flashes also attract prey to eat and warn predators that she won't taste good.

Now, a female **crested macaque** has a splendid backside. It tells other monkeys some tremendously important things about her. Any male can read her shiny hindquarters and tell when she last had a baby. So sometimes her bottom says to a male, "I'd like to be a mum." Sometimes it says, "Stay away."

I'd like to be a mum!

A **cuyaba dwarf frog** has what you might call 'the bottom line' in defence. If threatened, it turns around and shows the attacker its backside. What's more, it can puff up its bum so that it looks like a beastly pair of eyes! What a top-notch way of scaring off an attacker!

When a **wombat** comes out at night, it wants others to know it's there. So it poops up to 100 perfectly square cubes of poo, and leaves them carefully where they'll be seen. It's a fair and square way to say, "This is my patch!" It works a treat, because square poos don't roll off things as easily as round ones!

This **Fitzroy river turtle** is simply staggering. It can breathe with its bum! It sucks water into its back end, then absorbs the oxygen from it. This means these extraordinary little turtles can stay underwater for weeks at a time! They're endangered, though. Polluted water is no good for them. It doesn't have enough oxygen in it for the turtles to do their bum-breathing.

If you thought all those bums were fancy, a **sea cucumber** must have one of the most talented bottoms of all. Firstly, it breathes through it. Secondly, it shoots its guts out of it, to deal with predators. The intestines come out looking like strings of spaghetti and they form sticky nets that tangle up crabs and other creatures. Thirdly, it's got teeth on its bum which keep other animals from hiding inside!

Freaky Beaks

My beak is unique. I'm a **duck-billed platypus.**

You may think I go around with a shovel stuck on my face and, in a way, I suppose I do. But you won't get to glimpse it often because I'm shy. I hide in the water and come out at night.

I'm a mammal, but I've unkindly been called a freak of nature because I lay eggs like a bird and have a beautiful, duck-like beak.

In fact, my bill's flat shape helps me swim quickly. And it's perfect for scooping up insects, shellfish and worms from the water and mud of rivers and lakes. It also has an extra trick. It can sense electric signals made by the animals that I like to eat, which means I can find them in dark places!

So are we freaky, just because we're beaky? Just wait until you get an eyeful of some of my beautiful friends...

The **shoebill** has a funny name thanks to his whopping beak. But not only is it as tough as an old boot and shaped a bit like one, it gives him plenty of skills that others don't have. The sharp edges help him kill fish, and that hooked tip is perfect for gripping and crushing prey. It has spitting power too, for chucking out yucky plants and algae tangled around his food.

Size is everything for the **sword-billed hummingbird**. Her impossible-looking beak is longer than her body. She can reach delicious nectar at the end of the very long, tube-shaped flowers that other birds cannot get to. Her beak is no use for grooming, though. She has to do that with her feet!

You can see why this curious character is called a **parrotfish**. That's not a real beak, even though it looks and acts in a similar way. It's actually 1,000 teeth joined up in 15 tight rows. Parrotfish eat by chopping, crunching, grinding and scraping algae off hard corals. This daily chomping turns corals into fine sand, and over thousands of years it's helped to make beaches. Their toothy beaks are as hard as crystals.

Pointy at both ends, with a curling tail like a scorpion and a beak like a bird? It's a **scorpion fly**. With bizarre biting mouthparts you'd think he'd be a master at catching prey. But mostly he eats things that are already dead and, oddly, often uses his legs to pick food up. That beak is great for stealing insects from spider webs, though! And for offering food gifts to females.

Who's feeling greedy? A **pelican**'s bill is bigger than her belly! She dives down into water to hunt for fish. Then she uses her bill's pouch like a net, to scoop up fish and hold them safely away from other hungry birds. And she can drain the water from the pouch before swallowing her dinner.

Hungry **crested coua** chicks, and many other young birds, show their parents how lovely their beaks look inside. Every one has a unique pattern of decorations. These markings help the parents recognise each chick at feeding time. The patterns may be round, eye-like or in lines. Sometimes they even glow in the dark like little luminous pearls or coloured balls.

If you're going to sing, you may as well be loud and proud and wear a giant speaker, so everyone hears! That's what a **rhinoceros hornbill** does. His beak has a hollow 'casque' on top. It might look bonkers, but it acts like a clever echo chamber. His long beak also helps him pass food to his family. The mum nests with her eggs in a tree and the dad pokes snacks in through a tiny hole.

A **stink bug** has a beak for getting at hard-to-reach food. This beak has tiny spears on the tip for piercing plants, insects, birds, or mammals. The bug keeps it folded under its neck, swings it up to jab its prey, then pumps in saliva and sucks up its food. The beak falls off when the bug moults its skinlike exoskeleton. But it soon grows another.

Now here's a cool beak, literally. It belongs to a **toco toucan** and its true use has puzzled people for a long while. Toucans pick up fruit with their beak and toss it to the back of their throat. But their gigantic snapper is mostly used to cool themselves down in their hot tropical forest home. They do this by pumping blood in and out of their beak. It's great for impressing other toucans, too.

Extraordinary Eyes

You are deep in the jungle. It's the darkest hour of the night. Look into my eyes!

Do they send a tremble down your spine? Do they fill you with fear? Well, I hope not. Because there's really nothing spooky about a *tarsier's* eyes. They just make us masters of night-time hunting.

We don't have the special night-vision eyes that help many other nocturnal animals. Instead, we have absolutely huge eyeballs. Each of them is as big as our brain. They're so big we can't actually move them!

But with these super-sized, beady eyes we can spot grasshoppers, spiders and lizards hidden in the treetops. And we can pounce on them with deadly accuracy, by leaping through the darkness!

Are we the only ones with extreme eyes?

No, we're not...

An adult **emperor dragonfly** has enormous eyes wrapped around most of its head. With thousands of tiny lenses in each eye, it can see in all directions at once. Since this speedy super-vision is combined with split-second reactions, nothing can creep up on a dragonfly. This makes it a fearsome hunter of flying insects such as midges, mosquitoes, butterflies and moths.

This is an **amber snail** that has accidentally eaten the eggs of a green-banded broodsac worm. Sometimes they're nicknamed 'zombie snails'. The worm is a parasite. It lives inside the snail's tummy and makes its eyes pulsate in different colours. Flashing eyes mean the snail is likely to be eaten by a bird. And the worm wants that. Then it can lay its eggs in a bird's tummy. The eggs will be pooped out by the bird, for other snails to eat.

How would you like to have eyes on the back of your head? Many arachnids, such as this **jumping spider**, do. You need swift vision when you're hunting for speedy insects. And this isn't a problem for spiders, which have up to four pairs of eyes arranged around their heads. Each of them does a different job. Some pairs spot movement, some are for hunting, others are for finding a mate.

A **scallop** has two rows of bright blue eyes on the edges of its shell. There are up to 200 eyes on some types of scallop. These shellfish constantly keep watch for movement and changes in light, which may be the sign of an approaching predator. When they see danger, they snap their shells shut.

Here's a **spectacled owl**, and she definitely doesn't need glasses. Her wide eyes make her an expert hunter in the dark. Like other owls, she doesn't have eyeballs but long, light-catching tubes, a bit like binoculars. Eyes this shape work astonishingly well. They don't move in their sockets, but owls can swivel their heads almost a full circle to see what's behind them. And they bob about to look up and down. What's more, each eye has three eyelids which pop up, down and across!

When these Japanese **swallowtail butterflies** make babies, they join together backwards. To help with this, they have special 'eyes' on their bottoms! Many butterfly species have these. They can sense just enough light to make sure everything is in the right place. They also help female butterflies place their eggs on the right kind of plant.

Third eye!

This **blue iguana** has an amazing third eye on the top of her head. It looks up at the sky and can tell the iguana's brain many useful things. The third eye acts like a clock, a compass and a calendar. It also senses shadows of attackers overhead, telling her when to run away.

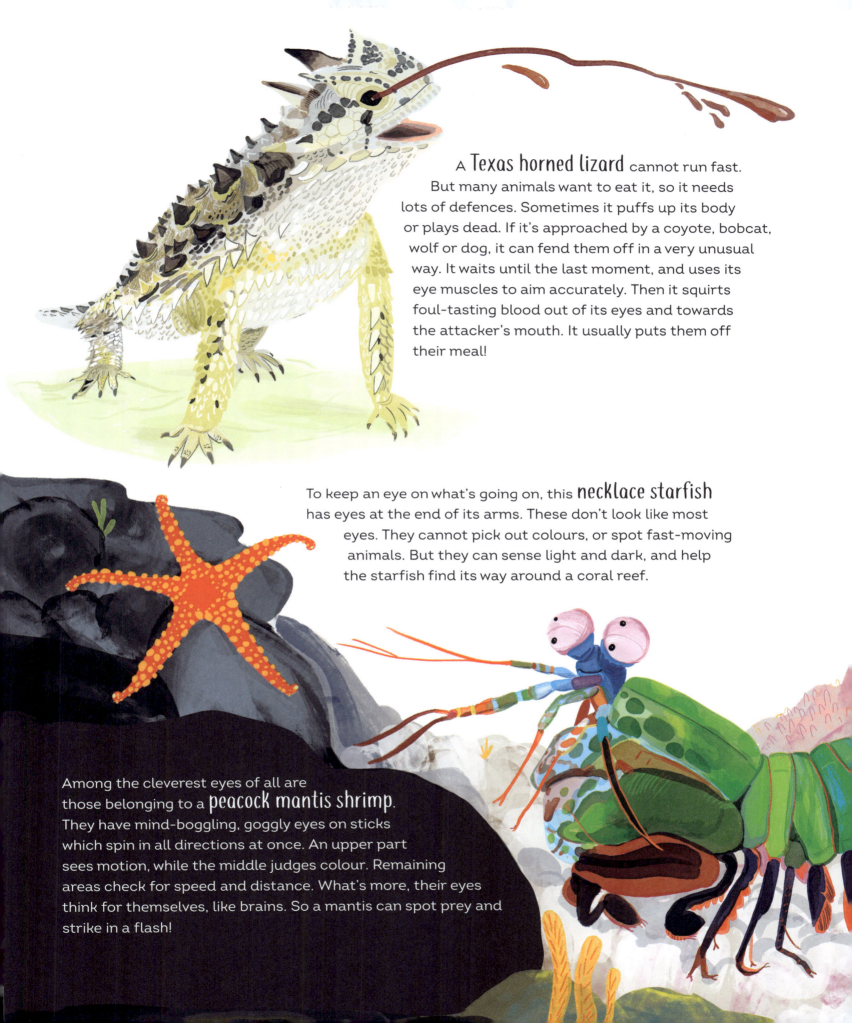

A **Texas horned lizard** cannot run fast. But many animals want to eat it, so it needs lots of defences. Sometimes it puffs up its body or plays dead. If it's approached by a coyote, bobcat, wolf or dog, it can fend them off in a very unusual way. It waits until the last moment, and uses its eye muscles to aim accurately. Then it squirts foul-tasting blood out of its eyes and towards the attacker's mouth. It usually puts them off their meal!

To keep an eye on what's going on, this **necklace starfish** has eyes at the end of its arms. These don't look like most eyes. They cannot pick out colours, or spot fast-moving animals. But they can sense light and dark, and help the starfish find its way around a coral reef.

Among the cleverest eyes of all are those belonging to a **peacock mantis shrimp**. They have mind-boggling, goggly eyes on sticks which spin in all directions at once. An upper part sees motion, while the middle judges colour. Remaining areas check for speed and distance. What's more, their eyes think for themselves, like brains. So a mantis can spot prey and strike in a flash!

Perplexing Necks

The animal kingdom is full of beautiful sights. But I doubt you'll find anything as handsome as a **wild turkey's** neck — especially mine.

I have all sorts of extra flesh around my face. There's a mass of skin under my neck called a wattle. I have wrinkled caruncles along the top of my head. There's a stylish red scarf of lumps round my lower neck called major caruncles. And this isn't to mention the snood that grows on my beak.

These fine-looking features don't just make us look magnificent. They serve a purpose. Male turkeys fight to decide a pecking order. And when we do, we pull at the leathery parts around each other's necks, and may even eat them!

Females prefer a mate with eye-catching dangly bits. And if I'm in the mood to attract a female, I can turn my flaps bright red.

So don't be perplexed. Sit back and let me tell you about some incredible necks...

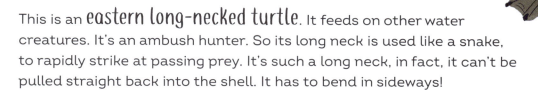

This is an **eastern long-necked turtle**. It feeds on other water creatures. It's an ambush hunter. So its long neck is used like a snake, to rapidly strike at passing prey. It's such a long neck, in fact, it can't be pulled straight back into the shell. It has to bend in sideways!

A **frilled lizard** has a fancy collar on her neck. Most of the time this lies folded away. But if frightened by a predator, this reptile will spread out the frilly skin to make herself look bigger than she is, and open her brightly coloured mouth. The startled predator is stopped in its tracks. And this gives the lizard the time she needs to gallop off and find somewhere safer.

Tadpoles are often eaten by fish, insects or snakes, which means they don't grow into frogs. But a father **Darwin's frog** offers his young some extra help. He gulps the eggs into his mouth and stores them inside a special part of his neck. They hatch into tadpoles in there, and he protects them for around six weeks. Good old Dad doesn't eat during all that time! His babies hop out through his mouth when they're bigger and better able to look after themselves.

A **great frigatebird** has a patch of skin below its neck called a gular sac. In males, this skin is red and it is inflated when they want to attract a mate. Gangs of them sit in trees, forcing air into their gular sacs and blowing them up like balloons! Then, as females fly overhead, the males waggle their heads and call out to get noticed.

This neck is almost as stunning as a wild turkey's. (Though not quite!) It belongs to a **superb fan-throated lizard**. When they want to impress a female, they perch where they can be seen and flaunt their iridescent flaps. They also flash them about to keep other males away.

The **giraffe weevil** is a small insect. So why does it have such a long neck? It's mainly for fighting. Males use their super-necks to push and wrestle with each other, in the hope that they'll win and be chosen by a female. The extra length of their necks is also useful when it comes to folding leaves into nests.

He may only be small, but this male **Indian bullfrog** has worked out how to make one heck of a noise! He has a pair of speakers on his neck. His big, round bubbles are called vocal sacs. They blast out this croaky crooner's songs so powerfully they can be heard from several kilometres away. They also turn bright blue in the mating season, which is attractive to females.

A **swan** has up to 25 vertebrae bones in her neck – more than any other bird. With her long neck, a mute swan can stretch 1.5 metres down into water. So she can reach underwater plants, which are a big part of her diet. She also curves her impressive neck and half-raises her wings as a warning, when feeling threatened.

A **giraffe** has the same number of bones in its neck as a mouse does – but they're much bigger! With its remarkable neck, a giraffe can grow over 5.5 metres tall. And why would you want a neck that long? It means giraffes can reach higher than other animals and get to tasty leaves in the treetops. It also helps them reach down to drink. And from high up, they can see predators when they're still far away.

A **king vulture** has mainly white and black feathers. But its neck is coloured orange, yellow and purple and has no feathers at all. Other vultures find the bright colours attractive. The bald neck helps keep these birds clean and healthy. King vultures feed on the corpses of dead animals and need bare necks to keep down the amount of bacteria they pick up when they eat.

Weird Ears

You're lucky if you notice a **spotted bat**. We fly at night and hang out in dark places like forests, caves and batty old buildings.

Children can hear some bats, but most adults can't. We actually scream louder than a rock concert. But we call at very high sound frequencies, which many animals don't hear. It's so loud we have to squeeze shut muscles in our ears so we don't deafen ourselves!

My enormous ears swivel and wiggle and can pick up the soft flutter of moth wings. When I fly, I use echolocation. I make calls that bounce around, and my ears turn the information into a sound map. That way I can 'see' in the dark! When I rest, I fold my ears away. I uncurl them again when it's time to hunt.

The world is full of creatures with remarkable ears. Here are some of my favourites...

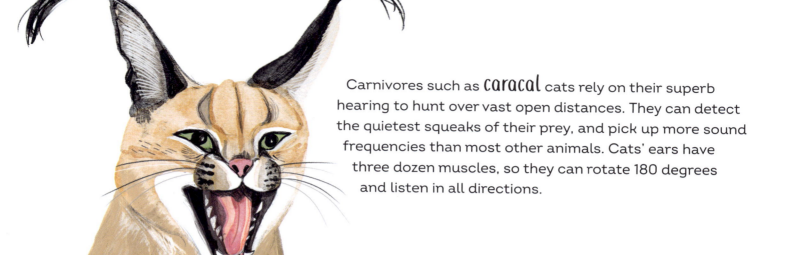

Carnivores such as **caracal** cats rely on their superb hearing to hunt over vast open distances. They can detect the quietest squeaks of their prey, and pick up more sound frequencies than most other animals. Cats' ears have three dozen muscles, so they can rotate 180 degrees and listen in all directions.

An **African bush elephant**'s ears are the biggest in the world and can hear sounds several kilometres away. They pick up vibrations of stampeding animals and know if predators are near. Ears this big also act as fans to cool them down in baking heat. And when they bathe, wet ears help them lose heat from their bodies. They also flap them to let each other know feelings of anger or joy.

Ear!

The **Australian spotted katydid** has ears on its legs! They are just below its 'knees' and they detect the clicks of hunting bats as well as the songs of possible mates. These animals catch prey by tricking male cicadas with a song that sounds exactly like a female's. To do this they have to copy a complex musical pattern very well. So they need good ears!

A **blue whale's** ears are hidden inside its head and are incredibly small, considering this is the biggest mammal on Earth. Even so, it has excellent hearing. It can pick up songs and the sound of other whales bellowing from hundreds of kilometres away. Whales don't need ears outside the body because sound travels so well in water. Their ears help them find food, navigate deep in the dark of the ocean and pick up warnings of danger. Whales also pick up sound through their skulls, jaws and air pockets in their heads. Their ears are stuffed full of ear wax, which acts a bit like a hearing aid.

The so-called 'ears' that the **dumbo octopus** is named after are actually flaps of flesh that help it move around. Each one has a water syphon inside, which the animal uses to steer and hover. Some octopuses can feel sound waves. So they do use a sense similar to hearing to listen for predators and catch prey. But this isn't done with a giant pair of dumbo ears!

If you live in a desert, you need to stay cool. A **jackrabbit** does this, thanks to gigantic ears that let off heat. This trick works best in the shade, where the air is cooler than its body. It pumps warm blood into its ears so heat can escape. And those sharp ears have superpower hearing, which is vital, because lots of hungry animals chase jackrabbits.

In autumn and winter, **red squirrels** grow fluffy red ear tufts. This fur falls out again during spring. Long, hairy ears help keep warmth in and water out during wet and chilly weather. They also help the squirrel hear predators coming, and they can be moved around to communicate a squirrel's mood. When feeling threatened, a red squirrel may raise or draw back its ear tufts, wave its tail and show its teeth.

What exceptionally big ears a **long-eared jerboa** has. They are longer than its head! In fact, they're the largest ears, relative to body size, in the animal kingdom. This little nocturnal desert rodent's special ears mean that it can hear predators from very far away and listen for insects to catch. The big ear surface also helps it cool down.

Many **butterflies** have 'ears' on odd parts of the body. Some have hollow tubes that look like veins on their wings. They pick up sound and carry it to special 'hearing organs', which are like tiny sacks of liquid wrapped on the body, below each wing. These 'ears' have nerves so finely tuned they can pick up high, ultrasonic calls of bats, the clicks of butterfly mates and the sounds of swooping birds.

A **long-eared owl** has brilliantly weird ears and a confusing name. Those tufts aren't ears at all. They're feathers. Her real ears are hidden on the sides of her head and, oddly, one is higher than the other. So sounds reach one ear a tiny bit faster than the other, and the difference tells the owl where a noise came from. She can judge the height and distance of even the quietest prey.

Terrific Teeth

My oddly-coloured **beaver** teeth aren't terrifying, they're terrific!

Teeth are great tools. That's why so many of us animals have them. We use them for getting food, and cutting and crushing it so it can be digested. Teeth are put on display to show who's boss. They're also a top defence against attackers.

My front teeth are rusty-orange because they contain lots of iron. It makes them extra strong. What's more, their backs wear down more quickly than their fronts, which makes them self-sharpening. They never stop growing, so they're just what beavers need for busy hours biting into trees. We strip bark to eat. Then we gnaw through trunks, topple trees and use them to build dams and lodges.

These clever constructions of ours change how rivers flow. They improve water quality, reduce flooding and make homes for fish, birds, bats, insects and frogs to share. All down to our mighty front choppers!

And we're not the only ones with tremendous teeth. Read on to discover others...

How about this for a special set of teeth? They belong to a **crabeater seal**. Just to confuse you, these seals don't eat crabs! They're experts at catching tiny crustaceans called krill. The unique pattern of their teeth works like a sieve. They gulp mouthfuls of seawater. The water escapes through gaps in their teeth, but any krill are trapped and eaten.

The **Pacific lamprey** has swum rivers and seas since before the days of the dinosaurs. It has a disk-shaped mouth lined with teeth, and feeds by attaching itself to a fish or whale. Then it uses its teeth and tongue to help itself to some of the other creature's blood. When mating, their vacuum cleaner mouths are useful in a different way. Lampreys use them to move stones and build underwater 'nests' for laying eggs.

A **gharial's** narrow snout cuts easily through water and its mouth contains more than 100 interlocking teeth. That many super-sharp biters is just what you need for snapping up fish and frogs. But, like other crocodilians, gharials can't use their teeth to chew. So they swallow stones to help mash up and digest their food.

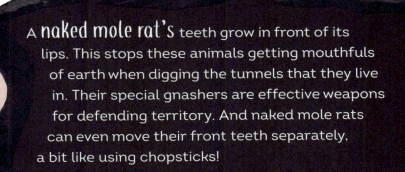

A **naked mole rat's** teeth grow in front of its lips. This stops these animals getting mouthfuls of earth when digging the tunnels that they live in. Their special gnashers are effective weapons for defending territory. And naked mole rats can even move their front teeth separately, a bit like using chopsticks!

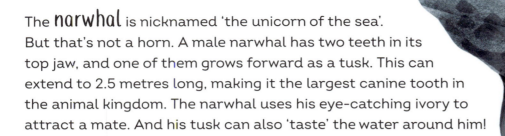

The **narwhal** is nicknamed 'the unicorn of the sea'. But that's not a horn. A male narwhal has two teeth in its top jaw, and one of them grows forward as a tusk. This can extend to 2.5 metres long, making it the largest canine tooth in the animal kingdom. The narwhal uses his eye-catching ivory to attract a mate. And his tusk can also 'taste' the water around him!

A **red demon squid** grows up to four metres long and has two powerful tentacles that grasp prey in a flash. It also has eight arms and its limbs are covered with 1,200 suckers, each ringed with 20 or more needle-sharp teeth. That's 24,000 teeth on each squid! The squid hunt together, sometimes in shoals of 1,000. So imagine an army of 24 million teeth jetting through the water, after their prey!

The tusks on a male **babirusa** are actually very long teeth. Two poke up out of the babirusa's mouth. Two grow down, curve round, pierce the roof of his mouth and stick out through the skin of his snout. The upper tusks are shields for defence. The lower ones are more like daggers and are used for attack.

A male **hippopotamus** has the longest teeth of any land animal. He grows them so he can fight off predators and other hippos. A special hinge on his jaw allows him to open his mouth to almost 180 degrees during displays. This reveals scarily sharp gnashers up to 50 centimetres long.

A **pygmy slow loris** is one of a few mammals with a 'toothcomb'. Several front teeth face outwards, so when these animals lick themselves clean, they comb their fur. A toothcomb is also handy for scraping resin from trees. And a mother slow loris even uses it to spread poisonous saliva onto her babies. That helps keep off parasites.

Venomous snakes, such as this **gaboon viper**, have fangs connected to venom glands. These are for hunting and defence. A viper's deadly biters are hollow, like the needles used for injections. Poison travels through them, into the victim. This paralyses prey, making it easier to swallow. At up to five centimetres long, the gaboon viper has the longest known fangs of any snake. And it's got a handy ability to fold them away when not in use!

This **sand tiger shark** has around 90 teeth. Because she bites hard on prey and shakes it about, a tooth often comes loose. But that's not a problem. Sharks have multiple rows of teeth and they're not rooted in their jaws. They're attached to skin. So new teeth move forward and replace ones that are lost. Sharks get through thousands of chompers in a lifetime. Their teeth are often washed up on beaches.

Peculiar Tongues

We sun bears are famous for our tongues.

We're the smallest of all bears, but our tongues dangle down a quarter of our height!

Now, why would we want tongues that look as if they've been borrowed from animals twice our size? Is it to make us look stylish? No. It's because they're fantastically useful!

A tongue like this is just what you need to scoop beetles from cracks in trees, lick termites out of hollows and poke grubs from rotten logs. We can use it to suck up juicy fruits. Then, if we find a wild bees' nest up a tree, what could be better than a super-long tongue for lapping up honey and young bees?

One other thing... it's pretty handy for grooming the parts of us that are hard to reach!

I'm not the only one with a cool kind of tongue. Check out this crazy collection...

Do you like these funky colours? They belong to a **San Francisco garter snake**. His tongue is pretty awesome, too. He loves to eat up frogs and newts. But that tongue isn't for tasting – it's for sniffing out where his prey is hiding. A forked tongue smells the air in two directions. This tells a garter snake whether its next meal is to the left or to the right. They also use this clever tongue trick to track down a possible mate.

A **giant anteater** has a tiny mouth and can barely move its jaws. So how does it eat? It's all about a bendy-straw tongue that goes deep into termite mounds and ant nests. It is covered in spines and sticky saliva, and is so good at its job that an anteater can swallow 30,000 insects in a day. Ants fight back by stinging, so anteaters have to be quick. They flick their tongues in and out more than a hundred times a minute, and they don't stay more than a couple of minutes at each nest.

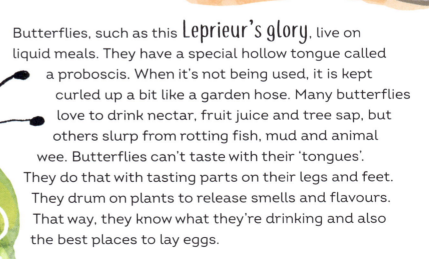

Butterflies, such as this **Leprieur's glory**, live on liquid meals. They have a special hollow tongue called a proboscis. When it's not being used, it is kept curled up a bit like a garden hose. Many butterflies love to drink nectar, fruit juice and tree sap, but others slurp from rotting fish, mud and animal wee. Butterflies can't taste with their 'tongues'. They do that with tasting parts on their legs and feet. They drum on plants to release smells and flavours. That way, they know what they're drinking and also the best places to lay eggs.

American flamingos, like some other birds, have tongues with pointy teeth running along both edges. These little gnashers grip food and move it to the flamingo's throat. The bird's special tongue is sharp enough to rip through plants and living prey. It also acts like a sieve, so flamingos can filter food from mud and water.

You'll love the tremendous tongue of a **Sumatran tiger**, but you might not want her to lick you with it! It's smothered in hundreds of backwards-pointing barbs. These mean this cool cat can scrape away the fur, feathers and every last scrap of flesh on her prey. Her multi-talented tongue also helps heal wounds and is purrrfect for combing dirt from her fur. Luckily, she can always flatten the barbs if she wants to give a friendly lick to a family member.

And who's this, sticking out his tongue at you? It's a **blue tongued lizard**. They're cold blooded, so they can't move fast unless they've warmed up. This means trouble if there are predators about, and that's where the freaky tongue comes in. A warning hiss and a flash of electric blue tongue startles predators. But it's just a trick! The blue colouring is actually harmless.

A chameleon's tongue sits curled like a piece of elastic inside its mouth until it gets fired out like a catapult! Smaller chameleons have the fastest tongues. Bigger ones, like this **panther chameleon**, have the longest. Either way, sticky slime and a suction pad on the tip of the tongue gives prey little chance of escape. A cunning, camouflaged chameleon catches a meal simply by waiting for a smaller animal to pass by – then ambushing it with a high-speed tongue attack!

Orchid bees come in groovy colours and their tongues are even groovier. They can stretch twice the length of their bodies. With such remarkable tongues, these bees can reach the deepest stores of nectar in the trickiest shaped flowers. And they'll buzz from flower to flower for up to 20 kilometres a day. The males aren't just looking for nectar, either – they collect perfume from flowers to impress females.

This scaly mammal is a **pangolin**. Its tongue can be 40 centimetres long, and even longer than its body! It's perfect for catching insects, but how does the pangolin fit it inside its mouth? The answer is, it doesn't. A pangolin's tongue starts right down at its bottom ribs. So, when it's not being used, its tongue is in its chest.

Who's Missing?

There's one extraordinary animal not yet mentioned. It's the human being — your species.

Humans have many incredible creature features. We have tongues that talk complicated languages. We have fingers and thumbs that can do skilful things, like make tools and play music.

And most extraordinary of all, we have big brains that work in ways no other animal's can. We've used our super-clever brains to develop technology, transport, science, art, stories and ways of sharing them around the world. We no longer grow fur all over our bodies to keep us warm, but we're intelligent enough to be the one animal that uses fire to stay warm and makes and wears clothes.

But are we quite as smart as we think? The cleverer we've tried to be, the more we seem to destroy wildlife around us. One million of the eight million wonderfully diverse species living on Earth are at risk of extinction because of humans. And this includes many of the amazing animals in this book.

Would a truly clever species be destroying the wildlife and ecosystems needed to support life in its one and only home?

It doesn't have to be like that. You have special human features. You can use them to care for wildlife, to share your love of wildlife with others, to learn more about our amazing animal cousins and find ways to help them survive and thrive.

Find Out More

If you'd like to find out more about how to help wildlife near you, or what is being done to protect endangered species, take a look at these organisations:

Buglife
www.buglife.org.uk

A UK charity standing up for the tiniest animals that run the world, from worms to spiders to pollinators. The website offers lots of ideas and activities for children to get involved in conservation and discover more.

Oceana
www.oceana.org/marine-life

Oceana is a global foundation that campaigns to protect the world's sea animals. The website is packed with facts about sea creatures, including some of the ones in this book.

PTES
www.ptes.org/kids-gone-wild

The People's Trust for Endangered Species (PTES) wildlife charity works to save some of our most at-risk animals and plants, and offers learning resources for children and an online Kids' Club.

RSPB
www.rspb.org.uk/fun-and-learning

The Royal Society for the Protection of Birds (RSPB) works on wildlife conservation in the United Kingdom. The website has lots of wildlife activity suggestions and ways to protect and explore nature.

Wildlife Watch
www.wildlifewatch.org.uk

Wildlife Watch is a website for kids, run by The Wildlife Trusts. It provides lots of wildlife information, fun activities, quizzes and details of nature reserves and wildlife events.

WWF
www.wwf.org.uk/learn/love-nature

The World Wildlife Fund (WWF) is a conservation organisation working to make the world a better place where people and wildlife can thrive together.